- You can never make your dreams come true by oversleeping.

- The best way to make your dreams come true is to wake up.

- Action should not be confused with haste.—Lee Iacocca

- Even if you're on the right track you'll get run over if you just sit there.—Will Rogers

- People may doubt what you say, but they'll always believe what you do.

- You'll never get a hit until you get the bat off your shoulder.—C. M. Ward

- The thing to try when all else fails is *again*. Giving it another try is better than an alibi.

- Everything comes to him who hustles while he waits.—Thomas Edison

- Roadside sign in Kentucky: "Pray for a good harvest, but keep on hoeing!"

Advice

A fool thinks he needs no advice, but a wise man listens to others.

PROVERBS 12:15

Wise & Wacky Wit

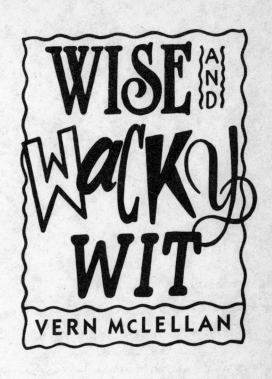

WISE AND WACKY WIT

VERN MCLELLAN

Living Books®

TYNDALE HOUSE PUBLISHERS, INC.
Wheaton, Illinois

Library of Congress Catalog Card Number
ISBN 0-8423-8249-6

Printed in the United States of America
98 97 96 95 94 93 92
 8   7   6   5   4   3   2   1

Contents

Accomplishment

If you wait for perfect conditions, you will never get anything done . . . . Keep on sowing your seed, for you never know which will grow—perhaps it all will.

ECCLESIASTES 11:4, 6

- After all is said and done, there's more said than done.

- Progress always involves risk; you can't steal second base and keep your foot on first.
  —Frederick Wilcox

- We are judged by what we finish, not by what we start.

- You can't build your reputation on what you're going to do.—Henry Ford

- The three great essentials to achieve anything worthwhile are first, hard work; second, stick-to-itiveness; and third, common sense.
  —Thomas Edison

- If God simply handed us everything we wanted, he would be taking from us our greatest prize—the joy of accomplishment.

- Every man who is high up loves to think that he has done it all himself; and his wife smiles and lets it go at that.—James Barrie

- He who putters around winds up in the hole.

- When your adversaries tell you that you can't go any farther, just tell them to look behind you and see how far you've come.

Action

Dreaming instead of doing is
foolishness, and there is ruin
in a flood of empty words.

ECCLESIASTES 5:7

- The reason God made woman last was that he didn't want any advice while creating man.

- If you are old, give advice; if you are young, take it.

- Most people want to serve God—but only in an advisory capacity.

- The boss looks on me as a sort of consultant; he told me when he wants my advice, he'll ask for it.

- The way to be successful is to follow the advice you give to others.

- Good advice is no better than poor advice, unless you follow it.

- Advice is least heeded when most needed.

- The trouble with giving advice is that people want to repay you.

- Advice to men over fifty: Keep an open mind and a closed refrigerator.

- "Be yourself" is about the worst advice you can give to some people.

Anger

A wise man restrains his
anger and overlooks insults.
This is to his credit.

PROVERBS 19:11

- People who fly into a rage will always make a bad landing.—Will Rogers

- When angry, count ten before you speak; if very angry, count a hundred.—Thomas Jefferson

- Anger is just one letter short of danger.

- Anger is the wind that blows out the lamp of intelligence.

- Anger gets us into trouble; pride keeps us there.

- Some people are like buttons—always popping off at the wrong time.

- The greatest remedy for anger is delay.

- For every minute you are angry you lose sixty seconds of happiness.

- Speak when you are angry and you'll make the best speech you'll ever regret.

- The best way to get rid of a hothead is to give him the cold shoulder.

- Anger makes your mouth work faster than your mind.

Argument

There's no use arguing with a fool. He only rages and scoffs, and tempers flare.

PROVERBS 29:9

Yanking a dog's ears is no more foolish than interfering in an argument that isn't any of your business.

PROVERBS 26:17

- To avoid a hot argument, keep a cool head.

- There are usually two sides to every argument, but no end.

- The only people who listen to both sides of an argument are the neighbors.

- When arguing with a fool, be sure he isn't doing the same thing.

- Arguments provide plenty of heat but little light.

- Even women find it difficult to argue with a man who won't talk.

- An argument occurs when two people try to get the last word in first.

- Before you have an argument with your boss, you'd better take a look at both sides—his side and the outside.

- Discussion is an exchange of knowledge; argument is an exchange of ignorance.

- After winning an argument with his wife, the wisest thing a man can do is apologize.

Association

There are "friends" who pretend to be friends, but there is a friend who sticks closer than a brother.

PROVERBS 18:24

- If you lie down with dogs, you'll get up with fleas.

- He who walks with a lame man will learn to limp.

- Character and ideals are catching. When you associate with men who aspire to the highest and best, you expose yourself to the qualities that make men great.

- He who enters a mill comes out covered with flour.

- If you want to soar with eagles you must avoid running with turkeys.

- It is better to be alone than in bad company.
  —George Washington

- The thing that counts most in the pursuit of happiness is choosing the right traveling companion.

- Tell me thy company, and I will tell thee what thou art.—Cervantes

- He who keeps company with a wolf will learn to howl.

Atheism

That man is a fool who says
to himself, "There is no God!"
PSALM 14:1

- Don't become an atheist—you'll have no holidays!

- An atheist is a man who has no invisible means of support.—Fulton J. Sheen

- An atheist is one who says he enjoys nature but does not know whom to thank.

- There are no atheists in foxholes.

- Sign on an atheist's tomb: "Here lies an atheist—all dressed up and no place to go!"

- They have all sorts of new services today. Now they've got a dial-a-prayer service for atheists. You call a number and no one answers.

- Atheists are really on the spot: they have to sing, "Hmmmmmmm Bless America."

- By night an atheist half believes in God.—Thomas Fuller

- The atheist cannot find God for the same reason a thief cannot find a policeman.

- Merry Christmas to our Christian friends. Happy Hanukkah to our Jewish friends. To our atheist friends—good luck!

Attitude

A relaxed attitude lengthens a
man's life; jealousy rots it
away.

PROVERBS 14:30

- Two men look out through the same bars: one sees the mud, and one sees the stars.

- The most destructive acid in the world is found in a sour disposition.

- A stiff attitude is one of the phenomena of rigor mortis.—Henry Haskins

- Two bricklayers were asked what they were doing. The first replied, "I'm laying bricks"; the second responded, "I'm building a great cathedral." Same task—different perspective.

- I never did a day's work in my life—it was all fun. —Thomas Edison

- The person who always looks down his nose gets the wrong slant.

- Don't go around with a chip on your shoulder; people might think it came off your head.

- A good thing to remember,
    A better thing to do—
  Work with the construction gang,
    Not with the wrecking crew.

- In War: Resolution. In Defeat: Defiance. In Victory: Magnanimity. In Peace: Goodwill.—Sir Winston Churchill

Boredom

Don't talk so much. You keep putting your foot in your mouth. Be sensible and turn off the flow! When a good man speaks, he is worth listening to, but the words of fools are a dime a dozen.

PROVERBS 10:19-20

- Some people can stay longer in an hour than others can in a week.—William Dean Howells

- One woman to another: "A terrible thing happened again last night—nothing!"

- It is always dullest just before the yawn.

- Boredom comes into the world via laziness.

- A bore is a person who deprives you of solitude without providing you with company.

- The cure for boredom is curiosity. There is no cure for curiosity.—Ellen Parr

- Did you hear about the fellow who was reviewing the highlights of his life and fell asleep?

- A bore is someone who goes on talking while you're interrupting.

- A bore always lights up a room when he leaves.

- A speaker who doesn't strike oil in twenty-five minutes should stop boring.

- There's only one thing worse than a bore, and that's a bore with bad breath.

Common Sense

Have two goals: wisdom—
that is, knowing and doing
right—and common sense.
Don't let them slip away, for
they fill you with living
energy and bring you honor
and respect.

PROVERBS 3:21-22

- Common sense is very uncommon.—Horace Greeley

- Common sense isn't as common as it used to be. —Will Rogers

- Common sense is something everyone can use, yet the only thing not being advertised.

- Horse sense (another breed of common sense) vanishes when you begin to feel your oats.

- It takes a lot of horse sense to maintain a stable life.

- The ideal combination in traffic is to have the horse sense of the driver equal the horsepower of his car.

- No barber cuts his own hair.

- Common sense is the knack of seeing things as they are, and doing things as they ought to be done.—C. E. Stowe

- Common sense is in spite of, not the result of, education.

- A meowing cat won't catch a mouse.

Conceit

There is one thing worse than
a fool, and that is a man who
is conceited.

PROVERBS 26:12

- As a rule, the fellow who toots his own horn the loudest is in the biggest fog.

- He who brags he knows everything sleeps in a fool's hallway.

- He who pats himself on the back may dislocate his shoulder.

- The world's most conceited man is the one who celebrates his birthday by sending his mother a telegram of congratulations.

- The guy who falls in love with himself will have no competition.

- Conceit is what makes a foolish little squirt think he's a fountain of knowledge.

- A sure cure for conceit is a visit to the cemetery, where eggheads and boneheads get equal billing.

- The person who is all wrapped up in himself is overdressed.

- The self-made man has relieved his Creator of an embarrassing responsibility.

- He who says he knows all the answers most likely misunderstood the questions.

Conscience

A man's conscience is the Lord's searchlight exposing his hidden motives.

PROVERBS 20:27

- Conscience: something that feels terrible when everything else feels wonderful.

- Conscience is a playback of the still, small voice that told you not to do it in the first place.

- What the world needs now is an amplifier for the still, small voice.

- A good conscience is a continual Christmas.
  —Benjamin Franklin

- He who has a fight with his conscience and loses, wins!

- Living with a conscience is like driving a car with the brakes on.—Budd Schulberg

- Conscience is like a baby. It has to go to sleep before you do.

- Small boy's definition of *conscience:* Something that makes you tell your mother before your sister does.

- Conscience is that still, small voice that yells so loud the next morning.

Courage

Wait for the Lord, and he will come and save you! Be brave, stouthearted, and courageous.

PSALM 27:14

- He who lacks courage thinks with his legs.

- It takes courage to stand up and speak, as well as to sit down and listen.

- The wishbone will never replace the backbone.
  —Will Henry

- One man with courage makes a majority.
  —Andrew Jackson

- Success is never final. Failure is never fatal. It's courage that counts.—Coach John Wooden

- Courage is the ability to "hang in there" five minutes longer.

- Faint heart never won fair lady.

- A rabbit is not supposed to climb trees, but sometimes he must.

- Courage is fear that has said its prayers.

- It's not so much the size of the dog in the fight that counts, but the size of the fight in the dog.

- The test of tolerance comes when we are in the majority; the test of courage comes when we are in the minority.—Ralph Sockman

Criticism

If you profit from constructive criticism, you will be
elected to the wise men's hall
of fame. But to reject criticism is to harm yourself and
your own best interests.

PROVERBS 15:31-32

- The trouble with most of us is that we would rather be ruined by praise than saved by criticism.

- Two things are bad for the heart: running up stairs and running down people.—Bernard Baruch

- Critics are self-centered people who go places and boo things.

- He who throws dirt loses ground.

- Have you ever noticed that most knocking is done by folks who don't know how to ring the bell?

- Any fool can criticize, condemn, and complain —and most fools do.—Dale Carnegie

- If what they are saying about you is true, mend your ways. If it isn't true, forget it, and keep on going.

- Blowing out the other fellow's candle won't make yours shine any brighter.

- Criticism is like dynamite. It has its place, but should be handled only by experts.

- Never fear criticism when you're right; never ignore criticism when you're wrong.

Death

Don't look to men for help;
their greatest leaders fail; for
every man must die. His
breathing stops, life ends, and
in a moment all he planned
for himself is ended.

PSALM 146:3-4

The good man finds life; the
evil man, death.

PROVERBS 11:19

- Did you hear about the undertaker who closed his letters with the words, "Eventually yours"?

- Most people agree that if you have to go, drowning in varnish provides the best finish.

- Secretary's dilemma: "Since I've used up all my sick days, I'm calling in dead!"

- Death: a path that must be trod, if man would ever pass to God.—Thomas Parnell

- Let us endeavor to so live that when we come to die, even the undertaker will be sorry.—Mark Twain

- Ninety-five percent of the people who died today had expected to live a lot longer.—Albert Wells, Jr.

- Death is not a period but a comma in the story of life.

- So live that when death comes the mourners will outnumber the cheering section.

- The saddest thing from birth to sod is a dying man who has no God.

Decisiveness

What a shame—yes, how
stupid!—to decide before
knowing the facts!

PROVERBS 18:13

- The answer is maybe—and that's final!

- If you don't stand for something, you'll fall for anything.

- A man should give a lot of thought before making a sudden decision.

- Almost everyone knows the difference between right and wrong; some people just don't like making decisions.

- An executive is a guy who can take as long as he wants to make a snap decision.

- New automobiles come equipped with a right-turn and a left-turn signal. What we need is one more—to indicate "undecided."

- Sign at the crossroads in a southwestern desert state: "Be careful which road you take—you'll be on it for the next 200 miles."

- No one learns to make right decisions without being free to make wrong ones.

- A decision is what an executive is forced to make when he can't get anyone to serve on a committee.

Determination

Steady plodding brings prosperity; hasty speculation brings poverty.

PROVERBS 21:5

- No man in the world has more determination than the one who can stop after eating just one peanut.

- Today's mighty oak is just yesterday's nut that held its ground.

- Some men succeed because they are destined to, but most men because they are determined to.

- Diamonds are chunks of coal that stuck to their job.

- Big shots are only little shots who kept on shooting.

- Prayer: "Lord, give me the tenacity and determination of a weed."

- Determined people begin their success where others end in failure.

- Behold the turtle. He makes progress only when he sticks his neck out.—James Conant

- When you get to the end of your rope, tie a knot and hang on.

- Satisfy your *want* and *wish* power by overcoming your *can't* and *won't* power with *can* and *will* power.—William Boetcher

Direction

Only a simpleton believes
everything he's told! A prudent man understands the
need for proof. A wise man is
cautious and avoids danger; a
fool plunges ahead with great
confidence.

PROVERBS 14:15-16

In everything you do, put God
first, and he will direct you
and crown your efforts with
success.

PROVERBS 3:6

- No wind is favorable for the sailor who doesn't know where he is going.

- If at first you don't succeed, try looking in the wastebasket for the directions.

- When all else fails, read the instructions.

- If you don't know where you're going, any road will get you there.

- The greatest thing in this world is not so much where we are, but in what direction we are moving.—Oliver Wendell Holmes

- It's more important to know where you're going than to see how fast you can get there.

- A wise man is like a tack—sharp and pointed in the right direction.

- Where you go hereafter depends on *what* you go after here.

- He who takes the wrong road makes the journey twice.

Discipline; Correction; Reproof

Punish a mocker and others
will learn from his example.
Reprove a wise man, and he
will be the wiser.

PROVERBS 19:25

A mocker stays away from
wise men because he hates to
be scolded.

PROVERBS 15:12

- Remember when a wayward child was straightened up by being bent over?

- When children start to sow their wild oats it's time for parents to start the thrashing machine.

- The prevention of crime begins in the high chair, not the electric chair.

- The behavior of some children suggests that their parents embarked on the sea of matrimony without a paddle.

- A pat on the back develops character if it is administered young enough, often enough, and low enough.

- Discipline yourself so others won't have to.

- One sure way to test your willpower is to see a friend with a black eye and not ask any questions.

- He who lives without discipline is exposed to grievous ruin.—Thomas à Kempis

Dreams

Hope deferred makes the heart sick; but when dreams come true at last, there is life and joy.

PROVERBS 13:12

- Did you hear about the fellow who dreamed he ate a five-pound marshmallow and when he awoke, his pillow was gone?

- The poorest of all men is not the man without a dollar, but the man without a dream.

- Some men see things as they are and say, "Why?" I dream things that never were and say, "Why not?" —George Bernard Shaw

- It doesn't do any harm to dream, providing you get up and hustle when the alarm comes on.

- Some people who think they are dreamers are just sleepers.

- You can never make your dreams come true by oversleeping.

- Castles in the air are OK until you try to move into them.

- People who are always walking on clouds leave too many things up in the air.

- Hitch your wagon to the stars, but keep your feet on the ground.

- Unless you try to do something beyond what you have already mastered, you will never grow. —Ronald E. Osborn

Drinking

Wine gives false courage;
hard liquor leads to brawls;
what fools men are to let it
master them, making them
reel drunkenly down the
street!

PROVERBS 20:1

- He who battles his way to the top too often bottles his way to the bottom.

- Hangover: the moaning after the night before.

- A pink elephant is a beast of bourbon.

- Stop and think before you drink.

- Cocktail party: A gathering where people drink martinis, spear olives, stab friends, and spill the beans.

- Boozers are losers.

- Booze-befuddled brains bring brawls, bumps, and bruises.

- A drinking man commits suicide on the installment plan.

- Traffic warning sign: "Heads you win—cocktails you lose."

- We drink to one another's health,
    And yet before we've finished
  Our round of toasts, our state of health
    Has noticeably diminished.

- Wife to husband with a hangover: "I don't see why your head should hurt this morning—you certainly didn't use it last night."

Driving

The man who strays away
from common sense will end
up dead!

PROVERBS 21:16

- The life of the party may become the death on the highway.

- Drive to arrive alive. It's smarter to be a little late down here than too early up there.

- If you don't drive wisely, your present car may last you a lifetime.

- The only marks some drivers make in life are skid marks.

- If your children want to take driving lessons, don't stand in their way.

- He who weaves through traffic may wind up in stitches.

- Famous last words: "I wonder how fast this car will go?"

- Seat belts are not as confining as wheelchairs.

- If you don't like the way I drive, stay off the sidewalk!

- He who drives too fast into the next county may wind up in the next world.

- Thousands of nuts hold a car together—but one can scatter it all over the road.

Education

How does a man become wise? The first step is to trust and reverence the Lord! Only fools refuse to be taught. Listen to your father and mother. What you learn from them will stand you in good stead; it will gain you many honors.

PROVERBS 1:7-9

- Everybody is ignorant, only on different subjects.
  —Will Rogers

- Too many people don't let studying interfere with their education.

- If you think education is expensive, you ought to try ignorance.

- There is nothing more frightful than ignorance in action.—Goethe

- An education is what a father receives when he sits in on a conversation with a group of teenagers.

- Education covers a lot of ground, but it does not cultivate it.

- It's not only the *IQ*, but also the *I will* that's important in education.

- When your education is finished, so are you.

- It is a good thing for an uneducated man to read books of quotations.—Winston Churchill

- You must not enthrone ignorance just because there is so much of it.

Egotism

Don't praise yourself; let
others do it!

PROVERBS 27:2

- Some self-made men show poor architectural skill.

- The person who sings his own praise seldom gets the right pitch.

- The "ideals" of some people are "'I' deals."

- The egotist says, "Everyone has a right to my opinion."

- He's a very religious man—he even worships the ground *he* walks on.

- Egotism is the anesthetic that dulls the pain of stupidity.

- An egotist is a self-made man who's in love with his creator.

- Egotism: "I" strain.

- There's one nice thing you can say about egotists: they don't talk about other people.

- An egotist is a person who is me-deep in conversation.

- An egotist is a man who thinks that if he hadn't been born, people would have wanted to know why not.

Excuses

The lazy man won't go out and work. "There might be a lion outside!" he says. He sticks to his bed like a door to its hinges! He is too tired even to lift his food from his dish to his mouth! Yet in his own opinion he is smarter than seven wise men.

PROVERBS 26:13-16

- He who is good for making excuses is seldom good for anything else.—Benjamin Franklin

- An ounce of performance is worth a ton of excuses.

- It is soon going to be too hot to do the job it was too cold to do last winter.

- Excuses are the nails used to build a house of failure.—Don Wilder and Bill Rechin

- He who excuses himself accuses himself.

- One of the most laborsaving inventions of today is tomorrow.

- We are all manufacturers—making good, making trouble, or making excuses.

- Don't make an excuse; make an effort.

- When you don't want to do anything, one excuse is as good as another.

- The man who really wants to do something finds a way; the other man finds an excuse.

- Never give an excuse that you would not be willing to accept.

Facts

A rebel doesn't care about the facts. All he wants to do is yell. . . . Any story sounds true until someone tells the other side and sets the record straight.

PROVERBS 18:2, 17

- The hardest thing about facts is facing them.

- Facts do not cease to exist because they are ignored.—Aldous Huxley

- A hard-liner's admission: "My mind's made up! Don't confuse me with the facts!"

- He who wants to stop a red-hot argument should lay a few cold facts on it.

- Digging for facts is better mental exercise than jumping to conclusions.

- He might not be a liar, but let's just say that he lives on the wrong side of the facts.

- Get your facts first, and then you can distort them as much as you please.—Mark Twain

- A candidate running for congress hired two assistants: one to dig up the facts and the other to bury them.

- Facts do not change; feelings do.

- You can tell how many seeds are in an apple, but you cannot tell how many apples are in a seed.

- An ounce of fact means more than a ton of argument.

Friendship

Wounds from a friend are
better than kisses from an
enemy! . . . Friendly suggestions are as pleasant as
perfume.

PROVERBS 27:6, 9

- Real friends don't care if your socks don't match.

- Friends are people who stick together till debt do them part.

- The world needs more warm hearts and fewer hot heads.

- He who walks in when others walk out is a true friend.

- The best way to keep your friends is not to give them away.

- The best way to test a man's friendship is to ask him to go on your note. If he refuses, he is your friend.

- The fastest way to wipe out a friendship is to sponge on it.

- A good friend is like toothpaste—he comes through in a tight squeeze.

- If you want an accounting of your worth, count your friends.—Merry Browne

- Real friends are those who, when you've made a fool of yourself, don't feel that you've done a permanent job.

Future

The wise man saves for the future, but the foolish man spends whatever he gets.

PROVERBS 21:20

- The worst trouble with the future is that it seems to get here quicker than it used to.

- College registrar's notice: "Owing to unforeseen circumstances, our course entitled *Predicting Your Future* has had to be cancelled."

- Perhaps the best thing about the future is that it comes just one day at a time.

- One thing the future *can* guarantee—anything can happen.

- The future belongs to those who prepare for it.

- My interest is in the future because I'm going to spend the rest of my life there.

- Hats off to the past; sleeves up for the future.

- January 1: "I resolve to be optimistic about the future—if there is one!"

- The future is history with God—for he is omniscient.

- He gave her a smile with a future in it.

Goals

Wisdom is the main pursuit of
sensible men, but a fool's
goals are at the ends of the
earth!

PROVERBS 17:24

- Long-range goals keep you from being frustrated by short-term failures.

- Climb high, climb far; your aim the sky, your goal the star.

- Establish a goal for which you're willing to exchange a piece of your life.

- Goals—write them down; hang them up; and with God's help, watch them happen!

- He who aims at nothing is sure to hit it.

- Obstacles are those frightful things you see when you take your eyes off the goal.—Hannah Moore

- There's no point carrying the ball unless you know where the goal is.

- Aim high, but stay on the level.

- He who hasn't figured out where he's going is lost before he starts.

- The first two letters of the word *goal* spell it and tell where it's at.

- People who want to move mountains must start by carrying away small stones.

Gossip

Fire goes out for lack of fuel,
and tensions disappear when
gossip stops.

PROVERBS 26:20

A gossip goes around spread-
ing rumors, while a trustwor-
thy man tries to quiet them.

PROVERBS 11:13

- A gossip is a fool with a keen sense of rumor.

- People who gossip usually wind up in their own mouth traps.

- There's so much good in the worst of us, and so much bad in the best of us, that it hardly behooves any of us to talk about the rest of us.

- A rumor is about as hard to unspread as butter.

- Unfortunately, rumor goes round the world while truth is getting its boots on.

- A gossip is a person who will never tell a lie when the truth will do more damage.

- Gossip: peddling meddling.

- More people are run down by gossip than by automobiles.

- It isn't hard to make a mountain out of a molehill; just add a little dirt.

- Gossip is anything that goes in one ear and over the back fence.

Griping

Gentle words cause life and
health; griping brings discour-
agement.

PROVERBS 15:4

- If you can't be thankful for what you receive, be thankful for what you escape.

- If you have a sore throat, be thankful you're not a giraffe.

- "Whines" are the products of sour grapes.

- He who growls all day lives a dog's life.

- A man who sits in a swamp all day waiting to shoot a duck, but gripes if his wife has dinner ten minutes late, is a miserable soul.

- Those individuals who always are quick
  With specific complaints that they're citing
  Will back off immediately when they are asked
  To please submit them in writing.
  —Erica H. Stux

- There's always something to be thankful for. If you can't pay your bills, you can be thankful you're not one of your creditors.

- Be thankful for your problems. If they were less difficult, someone with less ability would have your job.

- It's the second thank-you that proves you are grateful.

- The deadline for all complaints was yesterday.

Happiness

My son, how happy I will be
if you turn out to be sensible!
It will be a public honor to me.

PROVERBS 27:11

Happy is the man with a level-
headed son; sad the mother of
a rebel.

PROVERBS 10:1

- Happiness is hiring a baby-sitter who's on a diet.

- Happiness is having a scratch for every itch.
  —Ogden Nash

- Happiness is a rebound from hard work.

- The roots of happiness grow deepest in the soil of service.

- The really happy guy is the one who can enjoy the scenery even when he has to take a detour.

- The road to happiness is always under construction.

- Bride's father to the groom: "My boy, you're the second happiest man in the world!"

- A small house will hold as much happiness as a big one.

- Genuine happiness occurs when a wife sees a double chin on her husband's old girlfriend.

- Happiness is like a potato salad—when shared with others, it's a picnic.

Honesty

Lies will get any man into trouble, but honesty is its own defense.

PROVERBS 12:13

- Regardless of policy, honesty is easier on the nerves.

- It takes an honest man to tell whether he's tired or just lazy.

- If you tell the truth, you don't have to remember anything.—Mark Twain

- So live your life that your autograph will be wanted instead of your fingerprints.

- The world will be a better place when the "found" ads begin to outnumber the "lost" ads in the newspaper.

- Always trust a fat man. He'll never stoop to anything low.

- An honest merchant is one who puts up a "going out of business" sign—and then goes out of business.

- Honesty: another virtue that is praised—and starves.

- Make yourself an honest man, and then you may be sure there is one rascal less in the world.
—Thomas Carlyle

Humility

Pride leads to arguments; be
humble, take advice, and
become wise.

PROVERBS 13:10

- Few things are as humbling as a three-way mirror.

- Humility is a strange thing; the moment you think you have it, you have lost it.

- One of the hardest secrets for a man to keep is his opinion of himself.

- Humility is like underwear—essential, but indecent if it shows.—Helen Neilson

- Those traveling the highway of humility won't be bothered by heavy traffic.

- Humility is to make the right estimate of one's self.—Charles Spurgeon

- After crosses and losses men grow humbler and wiser.—Benjamin Franklin

- The fellow who has a good opinion of himself is likely a poor judge of human nature.

- There are two types of people in the world: those who come into the room and say, "Well, here I am!" and those who come in and say, "Ah, there you are!"

- The proud man counts his newspaper clippings— the humble man his blessings.—Fulton J. Sheen

Idleness

Hard work means prosperity;
only a fool idles away his
time.

PROVERBS 12:11

Idle hands are the devil's
workshop; idle lips are his
mouthpiece.

PROVERBS 16:27

- He did nothing in particular, and did it very well.—William Gilbert

- Office sign: "If you have nothing to do, don't do it here!"

- Idleness is only the refuge of weak minds, and the holiday of fools.—Lord Chesterfield

- People who have nothing to do are quickly tired of their own company.—Jeremy Collier

- The busy man is troubled with but one devil; the idle man by a thousand.—Spanish proverb

- Idleness travels very slowly, and poverty soon overtakes her.

- An idler is a guy who attempts to make both weekends meet.

- The man who has nothing to do, and gives it his personal attention, is an idler.

- Idleness: nothing to do and lots of time to do it in.

Knowledge

The simpleton is crowned
with folly; the wise man is
crowned with knowledge.

PROVERBS 14:18

- Some students drink at the fountain of knowledge—others just gargle.

- If you want to get into *Who's Who*, you'd better first learn what's what.

- No God, no peace; know God, know peace.

- Father to teenage son: "Maybe you should start shifting for yourself now while you still know everything."

- He who knows little too often shares it.

- The fellow who knows more than his boss should be careful to conceal it.

- The most underdeveloped territory in the world is under your hat.

- If there's a substitute for brains, it has to be silence.

- Horse sense shows itself when a fellow knows enough to stay away from a nag.

- Knowledge is not what the pupil remembers, but what he cannot forget.

Laziness

A wise youth makes hay
while the sun shines, but what
a shame to see a lad who
sleeps away his hour of opportunity.

PROVERBS 10:5

A lazy man sleeps soundly,
and he goes hungry!

PROVERBS 19:15

A lazy fellow has trouble all
through life; the good man's
path is easy!

PROVERBS 15:19

- The boss said to the lazy office boy: "Son, I don't know how we're going to get along without you, but starting Monday we are going to try."

- Most of this world's useful work is done by people who are pressed for time, tired, or don't feel well.

- He who rolls up his sleeves seldom loses his shirt.

- He's the kind of a guy with a Lincoln mind but a Pinto performance.

- "What parable do you like most?" the Sunday school teacher asked her class. Johnny was quick to reply, "The one about the multitude that loafs and fishes."

- Some people remind us of French bread—one long loaf!

- People who are the only breadwinners cannot afford to loaf.

- Sign in fast-food restaurant: "If you have time to lean, you have time to clean."

Leadership

I want those already wise to become the wiser and become leaders by exploring the depths of meaning in these nuggets of truth.

PROVERBS 1:5-6

Without wise leadership, a nation is in trouble; but with good counselors there is safety.

PROVERBS 11:14

Work hard and become a leader; be lazy and never succeed.

PROVERBS 12:24

- The trouble with being a leader today is that you can't be sure whether people are following you or chasing you.

- What this country needs is more leaders who know what this country needs.

- A real leader faces the music even when he doesn't like the tune.—Arnold Glasow

- He who stands at the head of the line must know where he's going.

- The person who follows the example of successful people avoids the trial and error of blazing his own trail.

- Lead, follow, or get out of the way.—Ted Turner

- Winning teams don't follow the leader; they take the lead.

- Football coach to high school team: "Remember, football develops individuality, initiative, and leadership. Now get out there and do exactly what I tell you!"

Listening

Come here and listen to me
[Wisdom]! I'll pour out the
spirit of wisdom upon you
and make you wise.

PROVERBS 1:23

- We have two ears and only one tongue in order that we may hear more and speak less.—Diogenes

- The first step to wisdom is silence; the second is listening.

- Husband calling his wife to the phone: "Dear, somebody wants to listen to you."

- A winner listens; a loser can't wait until it's his turn to talk.

- The only reason some people listen to reason is to gain time for rebuttal.

- Once a man learns how to listen he and his wife can remain on speaking terms indefinitely.

- Give every man thy ear, but few thy voice. —William Shakespeare

- There are two kinds of bores—those who talk too much and those who listen too little.

- Nothing makes a person such a good listener as eavesdropping.—Franklin Jones

- God still speaks to those who take the time to listen.

Love forgets mistakes; nagging about them parts the best of friends.

PROVERBS 17:9

- Love is oceans of emotions entirely surrounded by expanses of expenses.

- Did you hear about the nearsighted turtle that fell in love with an army helmet?

- Love is a form of insanity that makes a girl marry her boss and work for him for the rest of her life without salary.

- Ironic, isn't it, that in tennis, "love" is nothing, but in life, "love" is everything!

- You can give without loving but you can't love without giving.—Amy Carmichael

- A practical nurse is one who falls in love with a wealthy patient.

- A bell is not a bell until you ring it;
    A song is not a song until you sing it.
  Love in your heart is not put there to stay;
    Love is not love until you give it away.

- Love is an itch around the heart that's impossible to scratch.

- Better to have loved a short man than never to have loved a tall.

- Respect is what we owe; love, what we give.

- Love is the feeling that makes a woman make a man make a fool of himself.

Mistakes

A man who refuses to admit his mistakes can never be successful. But if he confesses and forsakes them, he gets another chance.

PROVERBS 28:13

- Never be dogmatic; we all make *misteaks!*

- The man who invented the eraser had the human race pretty well sized up.

- They used to say, "to err is human"; now they say it's the computer.

- Don't be afraid to ask dumb questions; they're easier to handle than dumb mistakes.

- A mistake is proof that at least somebody tried.

- To err is human, but when the eraser wears out before the pencil, don't you think you're overdoing it?

- He who claims he never made a mistake in his life generally has a wife who did.

- A well-adjusted person is one who makes the same mistake twice without getting nervous.

- Learn from the mistakes of others; you can't live long enough to make them all yourself.

Money

Don't weary yourself trying to get rich. Why waste your time? For riches can disappear as though they had the wings of a bird!

PROVERBS 23:4-5

- Money isn't everything, but it sure keeps you in touch with the children.

- Don't marry for money; you can borrow it cheaper.

- A person with money to burn will always have someone nearby with a match.

- Make all you can, save all you can, and give all you can.—John Wesley

- By the time some young people discover that money doesn't grow on trees, they're already out on a limb.

- For you can't take it with you,
  They've told me for years,
  And I've wisdom enough to perceive it.
  What's more, from the way that
  It's going, I doubt
  That I'll even be able to leave it.

- The best way to hear money jingle in your pocket is to "shake a leg."

- When we were kids, ten cents was big money. How dimes have changed!

- A collection has been defined as a church function in which many take but a passing interest.

- Money talks, but it doesn't say when it's coming back.

New Year's Resolution

I am still not all I should be,
but I am bringing all my ener-
gies to bear on this one thing:
Forgetting the past and looking forward to what lies
ahead, I strain to reach the
end of the race and receive
the prize.

PHILIPPIANS 3:13-14

- The New Year is like a new baby—many changes will be necessary.

- What the New Year brings to us will largely depend on what we bring to the New Year.

- Mark Twain once made the following New Year's resolution: "I'm going to live within my income this year even if I have to borrow money to do it."

- The trouble comes when the New Year's resolutions collide with the old year's habits.

- Habits are at first cobwebs, then cables.

- Habit is like a good bed; easy to get into but hard to get out of.

- A habit cannot be tossed out the window. It must be coaxed down the stairs a step at a time.—Mark Twain

- Keep your good habits and make new ones.

- A New Year's resolution is something that goes in one year and out the other.

- Another year older, another year wiser—oh well, one out of two isn't bad!

Obedience

God blesses those who obey
him; happy the man who puts
his trust in the Lord.

PROVERBS 16:20

- Teen Commandment: "Be smart, obey. You'll give orders yourself someday."

- He who cannot obey, cannot command.
  —Benjamin Franklin

- Resistance to tyrants is obedience to God.

- It is a great deal easier to do that which God gives us to do, no matter how hard it is, than to face the responsibilities of not doing it.—J. R. Miller

- Obedience to law is the largest liberty.

- Who says kids aren't obedient? They'll obey any TV commercial about buying a new toy.

- The time to teach obedience to authority is in the playpen instead of the state pen.

- It is our duty to obey God's Commandments (not suggestions!).

- Obedience is the sensible alternative for those who cannot lead.—Eugene Brussell

- Wicked men obey from fear; good men, from love.—Aristotle

Opportunity

As we have therefore opportunity, let us do good unto all
men.

GALATIANS 6:10, KJV

- An opportunist pulls himself up by *your* bootstraps.—Al Bernstein

- The sign on the door of opportunity says Push!

- The trouble with opportunity is that it's always more recognizable going than coming.

- There's no use going back for a lost opportunity; someone else has found it.

- Opportunity knocks, but it has never been known to turn the knob and walk in.

- The reason many people don't recognize opportunity is that it's usually going around disguised as work.

- The older you get, the longer it takes to get to the door if opportunity knocks.

- He who kills time buries opportunities.

- Opportunity knocks, but temptation kicks the door down. Opportunity knocks only once; temptation leans on the doorbell.

- An opportunist is someone who teaches the children to swim when the basement is flooded.

Patience

Be patient and you will
finally win, for a soft tongue
can break hard bones.

PROVERBS 25:15

- Be patient when people growl at you; they may be living with a bear.

- Patience is a virtue that carries a lot of wait.

- Patience is something you admire in the driver behind you and scorn in the one ahead.

- Living would be easier if men showed as much patience at home as they do when they're fishing.

- Did you hear about the fellow who wanted to be a doctor but he didn't have patience?

- Patience is the ability to count down before blasting off.

- If you are patient in one moment of anger, you will escape a hundred days of sorrow.—Chinese proverb

- Some people pray: "Lord, give me patience—right now!"

- Sign in a Texas country store: "Be patient. None of us am perfect!"

- They also serve who only stand and wait.—John Milton

- The horn of plenty is the one the guy behind you has on his car.—Crane

Peace

Fools start fights everywhere while wise men try to keep peace.

PROVERBS 29:8

- Sign in southern California psychiatrist's office: "Y'all Calm!"

- The only time I find peace is when I stop looking for it.

- Peace is the luxury you enjoy between your children's bedtime and your own.—Lester Klimek

- When at night you cannot sleep, talk to the Shepherd and stop counting sheep.

- The best way for a housewife to have a few peaceful moments to herself at the close of the day is to start doing the dishes.

- If there is righteousness in the heart, there will be beauty in the character.
  If there is beauty in the character, there will be harmony in the home.
  If there is harmony in the home, there will be order in the nation.
  When there is order in the nation, there will be peace in the world.
      —Chinese proverb

- Keeping peace in the family requires patience, love, and understanding—and at least two television sets.

- He that would live in peace and at ease must not speak all he knows nor judge all he sees.
  —Benjamin Franklin

Plans

Any enterprise is built by
wise planning, becomes
strong through common
sense, and profits wonderfully
by keeping abreast of the
facts.

PROVERBS 24:3-4

We should make plans—
counting on God to direct us.

PROVERBS 16:9

- Plan ahead—it wasn't raining when Noah began to build the ark!

- When you fail to plan, you plan to fail.

- He who plans his program for tomorrow takes confusion out of the day.

- God has no problems—only plans.—Corrie ten Boom

- Make long range plans as if you were going to live forever, and live today as if it were your last day on earth.

- The plans are man's; the odds are God's.—Chinese proverb

- Life is what happens while you're making other plans.

- There are four steps to accomplishment: Plan purposefully. Prepare prayerfully. Proceed positively. Pursue persistently.

- Failure is the path of least persistence.

- Light your lamp before night overtakes you.

Prayer

The Lord is far from the
wicked, but he hears the prayers of the righteous.

PROVERBS 15:29

- There will always be prayers in public schools—as long as there are final exams to take.—B. Norman Frisch

- Notice on high school bulletin board: "In the event of nuclear attack, all bans on prayer on this campus will be lifted!"

- He who is a stranger to prayer is a stranger to power.

- Seven days without prayer makes one weak.

- Pray to God, but row toward the shore.—Russian proverb

- Life is fragile, handle with prayer.

- He who spreads the sails of prayer will eventually fly the flag of praise.

- He who faithfully prays for rain should carry an umbrella.

- The quickest way to get back on your feet is to get down on your knees.

- If God is your Father, please call home.

- A teenager's view of prayer: "God answers prayer four ways: yes, no, wait awhile, or, you've got to be kidding!"

Preparation

A prudent man foresees the difficulties ahead and prepares for them; the simpleton goes blindly on and suffers the consequences.

PROVERBS 22:3

- Luck is what happens when preparation meets opportunity.—Elmer Letterman

- Chance favors the prepared mind.—Louis Pasteur

- Don't cross the bridge until you have the exact toll ready.

- Failure to prepare is preparing to fail.—John Wooden

- He who attracts luck carries the magnet of preparation with him.

- A college freshman wired home, "Mom, have failed everything! Prepare Pop."
  The reply came the next day: "Pop prepared! Prepare yourself!"

- Prepare and prevent instead of repair and repent.

- Prepare for eternity; you're going to spend a lot of time there.

- He who prepares today sets the stage for tomorrow's achievement.

Pride

If you have been a fool by being proud or plotting evil, don't brag about it—cover your mouth with your hand in shame.

PROVERBS 30:32

Pride leads to arguments; be humble, take advice, and become wise.

PROVERBS 13:10

Proud men end in shame, but the meek become wise.

PROVERBS 11:2

- If there is anything harder than breaking a bad habit it is to refrain from telling people how you did it.—Tony Pettito

- Temper is what gets most of us in trouble. Pride is what keeps us there.

- When a man gets too big for his britches, his hat doesn't fit either.

- People who are carried away by their own importance seldom have far to walk back.

- Success that goes to a man's head usually pays a very short visit.

- Always hold your head up, but be careful to keep your nose at a friendly level.

Priorities

In everything you do, put God first, and he will direct you and crown your efforts with success.

PROVERBS 3:6

Seek ye first the kingdom of God, and His righteousness; and all these things shall be added unto you.

MATTHEW 6:33, KJV

Honor the Lord by giving him the first part of all your income, and he will fill your barns with wheat and barley and overflow your wine vats with the finest wines.

PROVERBS 3:9-10

- Put God between you and everything.—F. B. Meyer

- He who puts God first will find God with him to the last.

- Do not have your concert first and tune your instruments afterwards. Begin the day with God. —James Hudson Taylor

- The first thing to do is fall in love with your work.

- If you do not knot your thread, you will lose your first stitch.

- Wise men learn more from fools than fools from wise men.—Cato

- We are silent at the beginning of the day because God should have the first word, and we are silent before going to sleep because the last word also belongs to God.—Dietrich Bonhoeffer

Problems

My only hope is in your love and faithfulness. . . . for problems far too big for me to solve are piled higher than my head.

PSALM 40:11-12

- Why can't problems hit us when we're seventeen and know everything?

- It's too bad that people can't exchange their problems; everyone knows how to solve the other guy's!

- Every problem parades as a possibility.

- For every problem God permits us to have, there is a solution.—Thomas Edison

- You must learn to pace yourself. Some problems weren't made to be solved—just worked on.

- The best way to solve your own problems is to help someone else solve his.

- Some people approach every problem with an open mouth.—Adlai Stevenson

- Problems are opportunities in work clothes. —Henry Kaiser

- If only men took the nation's problems as seriously as they do its sports!

- There is no problem that you and your heavenly Father can't handle.

- The right angle to approach a difficult problem is the "try-angle."

Promises

It is foolish and rash to make a promise to the Lord before counting the cost.

PROVERBS 20:25

As you enter the Temple, keep your ears open and your mouth shut! Don't be a fool who doesn't even realize it is sinful to make rash promises to God, for he is in heaven and you are only here on earth, so let your words be few.

ECCLESIASTES 5:1-2

- He who promises and gives nothing is comfort to a fool.

- Promises may get friends, but it is performances that keep them.

- The fellow who is the slowest in making a promise is the most faithful in keeping it.

- God promises a safe landing but not a calm passage.

- Your future is as bright as the promises of God.

- Vote for the man that promises least; he'll be the least disappointing.—Bernard Baruch

- The politician was full of promises that go in one year and out the other.

- Some people stand on the promises; others just sit on the premises.

Quarrels

As the churning of cream
yields butter, and a blow to
the nose causes bleeding, so
anger causes quarrels.

PROVERBS 30:33

It is hard to stop a quarrel
once it starts, so don't let it
begin.

PROVERBS 17:14

- In quarreling, the truth is always lost.—Publilius Syrus

- Very often a fight for what is right turns into a quarrel for what is left.

- Husband, during a quarrel: "You talk like an idiot!" Wife: "I have to talk like that so you can understand me."

- Quarrels would not last long if the fault was only on one side.

- Never pick a quarrel, even when it's ripe.

- When quarreling with a stupid person, be sure he isn't doing the same thing.

- Whether it's on the road or in an argument, when the color changes to red, *Stop!*

Questioning

Ask, and you will be given
what you ask for. Seek, and
you will find. Knock, and the
door will be opened.

MATTHEW 7:7

- He who asks a question may be a fool for five minutes, but he who never asks a question remains a fool forever.

- Asking saves a lot of guesswork.

- He who knows all the answers most likely misunderstood the questions.

- Four and twenty are the most desirable ages: at four, you know all the questions; at twenty, you know all the answers.

- Mother rabbit to her small child: "A magician pulled you out of a hat. Now stop asking questions!"

- Don't hesitate to ask stupid questions; they're easier to handle than stupid mistakes.

- There are two sides to every question, and to hold public office you have to be for both of them.

- After giving what he considered a stirring, fact-filled campaign speech, the candidate looked out at his audience and confidently asked, "Now, are there any questions?"
  "Yes," came a voice from the rear. "Who else is running?"

Reputation

If you must choose, take a
good name rather than great
riches; for to be held in loving
esteem is better than silver
and gold.

PROVERBS 22:1

A good reputation is more
valuable than the most expensive perfume.

ECCLESIASTES 7:1

- A good past is the best thing a man can presently use for a future reference.

- An open confession is good for the soul, but bad for the reputation.

- Associate yourself with men of good quality if you esteem your own reputation.—George Washington

- A good name, like good will, is attained by many actions and may be lost by only one.

- Many a guy gets a reputation for being energetic when in truth he's merely fidgety.

- Your reputation is made by searching for things that can't be done—and doing them.

- Character is what you really are; reputation is only what others believe you to be.

Responsibility

Riches can disappear fast. And the king's crown doesn't stay in his family forever—so watch your business interests closely. Know the state of your flocks and your herds.

PROVERBS 27:23-24

Young man, it's wonderful to be young! Enjoy every minute of it! Do all you want to; take in everything, but realize that you must account to God for everything you do.

ECCLESIASTES 11:9

- I have a very responsible job here; I'm responsible for everything that goes wrong.

- Wife: "I expect my husband to be just what he is now twenty years from today."
  Friend: "But that's unreasonable."
  Wife: "Yes, that's what he is now."

- Man blames most accidents on fate—but feels a more personal responsibility when he makes a hole-in-one on the golf course.

- When you take responsibility on your shoulders, there's not much room left for chips.

- Some people grow under responsibility, while others only swell.

- The game is my wife. It demands loyalty and responsibility . . . and it gives me back fulfillment and peace.—Michael Jordan

- Too many people confine their exercise to running up bills, stretching the truth, bending over backward, lying down on the job, sidestepping responsibility, jumping to conclusions, and pushing their luck.

Self-control

It is better to be slow-tempered than famous; it is better to have self-control than to control an army.

PROVERBS 16:32

- The best way to save face is to keep the lower part shut.

- Keep your mouth shut—and your IQ will go up.
  —Murray Pezim

- He who thinks twice before saying nothing is wise.

- The man who loses his head is usually the last one to miss it.

- He who talks without thinking runs more risks than he who thinks without talking.

- Be careful of your thoughts; they may break out into words at any time.

- He who thinks by the inch and talks by the yard deserves to be kicked by the foot.

- Poise is the act of raising your eyebrows instead of the roof.

- At no time is self-control more difficult than in a time of incredible conquest.

- If a man keeps his trap shut, the world will beat a path to his door.

Silence

The man of few words and settled mind is wise; therefore, even a fool is thought to be wise when he is silent. It pays him to keep his mouth shut.

PROVERBS 17:27-28

- A closed mouth catches no flies.

- Silence is evidence of a superb command of the English language.

- Talking comes by nature; silence by wisdom.

- He who is a man of silence is a man of sense.

- Silence is golden except when it comes to witnessing—then it's plain yellow.

- I have never been hurt by anything I didn't say. —Calvin Coolidge

- Some people won't suffer in silence; that would take the pleasure out of it.

- Silence is another thing that marriage brings out in a man.

- The hardest thing to keep is quiet.

- Silence is an awesome answer.

Success

Do you know a hard-working man? He shall be successful and stand before kings!

PROVERBS 22:29

- If at first you don't succeed—well, so much for skydiving.

- If at first you don't succeed, you're running about average.

- You don't have to lie awake nights to succeed, just stay awake days.

- The only place where success comes before work is in the dictionary.

- It takes twenty years to make an overnight success.—Eddie Cantor

- Success often comes from taking a misstep in the right direction.

- The secret of success is to be like a duck—smooth and unruffled on top, but paddling like crazy underneath.

- You will find the key to success under the alarm clock.

- He who wakes up and finds himself successful has not been asleep.

- God has given us two ends—one to think with and one to sit on. Your success depends on which one you use most.

- He who itches for success must be willing to scratch for it.

Tact; Diplomacy

A man is a fool to trust himself! But those who use God's wisdom are safe.

PROVERBS 28:26

- A diplomat can keep his shirt on while getting something off his chest.

- A diplomat remembers a lady's birthday but forgets her age.

- Tact is the art of making a point without making an enemy.—Howard Newton

- Diplomacy is the art of saying "Nice Doggie!" till you can find a stick.

- Diplomacy is the art of letting someone else have your way.

- A diplomatic husband said to his wife, "How do you expect me to remember your birthday when you never look any older?"

- Tact is changing the subject without changing your mind.

- A diplomat is a parent with two boys on different Little League teams.

- Tact is the art of making guests feel at home when that's where you wish they were.

- A diplomat is a gent who thinks twice before saying anything.

Talk

Don't talk so much. You keep putting your foot in your mouth. Be sensible and turn off the flow! . . . Those who love to talk will suffer the consequences. Men have died for saying the wrong thing!

PROVERBS 10:19; 18:21

- Some fools talk not because they have something to say, but because they have to say something.

- People who talk too much should vulcanize the leak below the nose.

- Superior people talk about ideas; mediocre people talk about things; little people talk about other people.

- Sign in office: "Be sure your brain is engaged before putting your mouth into gear."

- It is better to be quiet and look stupid than to talk and remove all doubt.

- It's not polite to talk with a full mouth or an empty head.

- He who talks too fast often says things he hadn't thought of yet.

- When you are in deep water, the best thing to do is keep your mouth shut.

- Jane: "What's the idea? You yawned seven times while I was talking to you."
  John: "No I didn't. I was just trying to say something!"

Teamwork

How wonderful it is, how
pleasant, when brothers live
in harmony!

Psalm 133:1

- Cooperate! Remember the banana? Every time it leaves the bunch it gets skinned.

- Cooperation determines the rate of progress.

- If you ever see a turtle on a stump, you know he didn't get there by himself.

- He who helps someone else up the hill gets closer to the top himself.

- My biggest thrill came the night Elgin Baylor and I combined for 73 points in Madison Square Garden. Elgin had 71 of them.—Rod Hundley

- He who pulls on the oars doesn't have time to rock the boat.

- You cannot applaud with one hand.

- One lights the fire, the other fans it.

- Who passed the ball to you when *you* scored?

- If a moron holds a cow by the ears, a clever man can milk her.

- If you wanna play hoop, you gotta do group.
  —Lonnie Wilson

Temper

Keep away from angry, short-tempered men, lest you learn to be like them and endanger your soul.

PROVERBS 22:24-25

A hot-tempered man stirs up dissension, but a patient man calms a quarrel.

PROVERBS 15:18, NIV

- Nothing will cook your goose faster than a red-hot temper.

- Your temper may get you into hot water, but it's stubbornness that keeps you there.

- My life is in the hands of any fool who makes me lose my temper.

- Funny thing about temper; you can't get rid of it by losing it.

- He who loses his head is usually the last one to miss it.

- He who loses his temper usually loses.

- About the time a man gets his temper under control he goes out and plays golf again.

- People who have an axe to grind often fly off the handle.

- Temperamental: 90 percent temper, 10 percent mental.

Time

O my son, whom I have dedi-
cated to the Lord, do not
spend your time with
women—the royal pathway
to destruction.

PROVERBS 31:2-3

- Six-thirty is my time to rise,
    But I'm seldom bright of eye;
  Part of me says, "Look alive!"
    And the other part asks, "Why?"

- Sign over college classroom clock: "Time will pass; will you?"

- Time is a versatile performer. It flies, marches, heals all wounds, runs out, and will tell.—Franklin Jones

- Why is there never enough time to do it right . . . and always enough time to do it over?

- If you must kill time, work it to death.

- Never try to teach a pig to sing; it wastes time and annoys the pig.

- If you think time heals everything, try waiting in a doctor's office.

- Dost thou love life? Then do not squander time, for that is the stuff life is made of.—Benjamin Franklin

- A great timesaver is love at first sight.

- He who kills time injures eternity.

- Time is so powerful that it is given to us only in small doses.

- Days are like suitcases. By careful arrangement, some people can pack more into them than others.

Tomorrow

But the good man walks
along in the ever-brightening
light of God's favor; the dawn
gives way to morning splen-
dor, while the evil man gropes
and stumbles in the dark.

PROVERBS 4:18-19

- The lazier a man is, the more he plans to do tomorrow.

- Defer not until tomorrow to be wise,
  For tomorrow's sun may never rise.

- Never put off until tomorrow what you can do today. If you wait until tomorrow, they will probably have passed a law prohibiting it.

- Tomorrow is usually the busiest day of the year.

- Did you hear about the fellow who faced his problems one tomorrow at a time?

- Procrastination is the art of keeping up to yesterday.

- Procrastination is the art of taking a long time to start to begin to get ready to commence.

- Yesterday is gone; forget it! Tomorrow never comes; don't wait for it! Today is here; use it!

Tongue

A wise man holds his tongue. Only a fool blurts out everything he knows; that only leads to sorrow and trouble.

PROVERBS 10:14

Self-control means controlling the tongue! A quick retort can ruin everything.

PROVERBS 13:3

- Your tongue is in a wet place—don't let it slip.

- The reason a dog has so many friends is because he wags his tail instead of his tongue.

- From a slip of the foot
    You may soon recover,
But a slip of the tongue
    You may never get over.
    —Benjamin Franklin.

- A tongue, three inches long, can kill a man six feet tall.—Japanese proverb

- A sharp tongue is no indication of a keen mind.

- Tongue twister: a phrase that gets your tang all tongueled up.

- A loose tongue often gets its owner into a tight place.

- He who has a sharp tongue eventually cuts his own throat.

Understanding

How much better is wisdom
than gold, and understanding
than silver!

PROVERBS 16:16

- There are two periods in a man's life when he doesn't understand women—before and after marriage.

- Frustrated husband: "All right, you don't understand me. I don't suppose Mrs. Einstein understood Albert either."

- A clever man tells a woman he understands her—but a stupid one tries to prove it.

- Little boy, after being scolded by his parents, said to his sister: "I'll never understand grown-ups if I live to be eight!"

- Humanity's greatest need is not for money, but for more understanding.

- Instead of putting others in their place, try putting yourself in their place.

- Understanding is the soil in which grow all the fruits of friendship.—Woodrow Wilson

- Most people are bothered by those passages in Scripture which they cannot understand; but as for me, I always noticed that the passages in Scripture which trouble me most are those which I do understand.—Mark Twain

Winning; Losing

So I run straight to the goal
with purpose in every step. I
fight to win. I'm not just
shadow-boxing or playing
around.

1 CORINTHIANS 9:26

- The loser says, "The worst is just around the corner." The winner says, "The best is yet to come."

- The road to success is always under construction.

- Winning isn't everything but wanting to win is.
  —Arnold Palmer

- Winning isn't everything, but it sure beats coming in second.

- Winners are people who aren't afraid to take a chance now and then. Losers sit around and wait for the odds to improve.

- The athlete was explaining his inner feelings. "Sometimes," he said, "it feels like I have two dogs fighting inside of me—one brown, the other white." "Which one wins?" he was asked. "The one I feed," he replied.

- Success comes in cans; failure comes in can'ts.

- Falling down doesn't make you a failure, but staying down does.

- Show me a man who is a good loser and I'll show you a man who is playing golf with his boss.

- Failure is the path of least persistence.

Wisdom

For the Lord grants wisdom!
His every word is a treasure
of knowledge and under-
standing.

PROVERBS 2:6

He who loves wisdom loves
his own best interest and will
be a success.

PROVERBS 19:8

- If ignorance is bliss, why aren't more people happy?

- Boyfriend: "If my girl said what she thought, she'd be speechless."

- Intelligence: Spotting a flaw in the boss's character. Wisdom: Not mentioning it.

- A wise husband will buy his wife such fine china that she won't trust him to wash the dishes.

- He who is wise by day is no fool by night.

- God grant me the serenity to accept the things I cannot change; the courage to change the things I can; and the wisdom to know the difference. —Reinhold Niebuhr

- The door of wisdom swings on hinges of common sense and uncommon thoughts.—William A. Ward

- A wise man will never plant more garden than his wife can take care of.

Words; Speech

From a wise mind comes careful and persuasive speech. A rebel's foolish talk should prick his own pride! But the wise man's speech is respected.

PROVERBS 16:23; 14:3

- Don't say anything you wouldn't be willing to write out and sign your name to.

- A perfect after-dinner speech is the shortest distance between two jokes.

- A good speech consists of a good beginning and a good ending—preferably close together.

- Out of the mouths of babes come words you never should have used in the first place.

- Most girls have a speech impediment; they have to stop to breathe!

- Be careful what you say in front of children. They are like blotters—they soak it all in and get it all backwards!

- The best ingredient in the recipe of public speaking is the shortening.

- As a vessel is known by its sound, whether it be cracked or not, so men are proved by their speeches whether they be wise or foolish.
  —Demosthenes

- A second wind is what some preachers get when they say, "And now in conclusion."

Work

Work brings profit; talk
brings poverty!

PROVERBS 14:23

- The harder you work, the luckier you get.—Gary Player

- Most people work for a good cause: 'cause they need the money.

- If you want a place in the sun, expect some blisters.

- Some people remind us of blisters; they show up after the work is done.

- The second laziest worker on earth is the guy who joins as many unions as possible to make sure he is always on strike.

- He who wants to make footprints in the sands of time must not sit down.

- Salesman: "This machine will cut your work in half." Customer: "Great! I'll take two!"

- He who rolls up his sleeves seldom loses his shirt.

- Too many people are ready to carry the stool when the piano needs to be moved.

- Work for the Lord. The pay isn't much, but the retirement is out of this world.

Worry

Such a man . . . . does not fear
bad news, nor live in dread of
what may happen. For he is
settled in his mind that
Jehovah will take care of him.

PSALM 112:6-7

- Blessed is the man who is too busy to worry in the daytime, and too sleepy to worry at night.

- Worry comes by human interference with the divine plan.

- Worry is like a rocking chair; it gives you something to do but it doesn't get you anyplace.

- Worry is the interest paid by those who borrow trouble.

- Wife to husband: "Seven o'clock, dear. Time to get up and start worrying!"

- A good memory test: What were you worrying about this time last year?

- Two days we should never worry about —yesterday and tomorrow.

- Worrying is a form of arguing with God.

- Elephants live longer than people. Maybe it's because they never worry about trying to lose weight.

- A woman was shocked when a friend mentioned that her husband's career lay in ruins. She was reassured: "Don't worry, he's an archaeologist."

Yesterday; Today

Teach us to number our days
and recognize how few they
are; help us to spend them as
we should.

PSALM 90:12

- No matter how you used yesterday, you received twenty-four hours today.

- Yesterday was such a bad day. My twin sister forgot my birthday.

- Yesterday's unfinished task is a mortgage on today.

- Yesterday's hits won't win today's ball game.

- Don't let yesterday use up too much of today.
  —Will Rogers

- Yesterday was the end of the line for a negative train of thought.

- Today's troubles are so often yesterday's unsolved problems.

- Between tomorrow's dream and yesterday's regret is today's opportunity.

- If you must cry over spilt milk, condense it.

Other Living Books Best-Sellers

74 MORE FUN AND CHALLENGING BIBLE CROSSWORDS. This brand-new batch of crosswords features both theme puzzles and general crosswords on a variety of levels, all relating to Bible facts, characters, and terms. 07-0488-6

400 CREATIVE WAYS TO SAY I LOVE YOU by Alice Chapin. Perhaps the flame of love has almost died in your marriage, or you have a good marriage that just needs a little spark. Here is a book of creative, practical ideas for the woman who wants to show the man in her life that she cares. 07-0919-5

ANSWERS by Josh McDowell and Don Stewart. In a question-and-answer format, the authors tackle sixty-five of the most-asked questions about the Bible, God, Jesus Christ, miracles, other religions, and creation. 07-0021-X

ANSWERS TO YOUR FAMILY'S FINANCIAL QUESTIONS by Larry Burkett. Questions about credit, saving, taxes, insurance, and more are answered in this handbook that shows how the Bible can guide our financial lives. 07 0025-2

THE BEST OF BIBLE TRIVIA I: KINGS, CRIMINALS, SAINTS, AND SINNERS by J. Stephen Lang. A fascinating book containing over 1,500 questions and answers about the Bible arranged topically in over 50 categories. Taken from the best-selling **Complete Book of Bible Trivia.** 07-0464-9

THE CHILD WITHIN by Mari Hanes. The author shares insights she gained from God's Word during her own pregnancy. She identifies areas of stress, offers concrete data about the birth process, and points to God's sure promises that he will gently lead those that are with young. 07-0219-0

CHRISTIANITY: THE FAITH THAT MAKES SENSE by Dennis McCallum. New and inquiring Christians will find spiritual support in this readable apologetic, which presents a clear, rational defense for Christianity to those unfamiliar with the Bible. 07-0525-4

COME BEFORE WINTER AND SHARE MY HOPE by Charles R. Swindoll. A collection of brief vignettes offering hope and the assurance that adversity and despair are temporary setbacks we can overcome! 07-0477-0

Other Living Books Best-Sellers

THE COMPLETE GUIDE TO BIBLE VERSIONS by Philip W. Comfort. A guidebook with descriptions of all the English translations and suggestions for their use. Includes the history of biblical writings. 07-1251-X

DARE TO DISCIPLINE by James Dobson. A straightforward, plainly written discussion about building and maintaining parent/child relationships based upon love, respect, authority, and ultimate loyalty to God. 07-0522-X

DR. DOBSON ANSWERS YOUR QUESTIONS by James Dobson. In this convenient reference book, renowned author Dr. James Dobson addresses heartfelt concerns on many topics, including questions on marital relationships, infant care, child discipline, home management, and others. 07-0580-7

GIVERS, TAKERS, AND OTHER KINDS OF LOVERS by Josh McDowell and Paul Lewis. Bypassing generalities about love and sex, this book answers the basics: Whatever happened to sexual freedom? Do men respond differently than women? Here are straight answers about God's plan for love and sexuality. 07-1031-2

HINDS' FEET ON HIGH PLACES by Hannah Hurnard. A classic allegory of a journey toward faith that has sold more than a million copies! 07-1429-6

HAVE YOU SEEN CANDACE? by Wilma Derksen. In this inspiring true story, Wilma Derksen recounts the hope and agony of the search for her missing daughter. Through Wilma's faith, readers will discover forgivness and love that overcome evil. 07-0377-4

THE INTIMATE MARRIAGE by R. C. Sproul. The author focuses on biblical patterns of marriage and practical ways to develop intimacy. Discussion questions included at the end of each chapter. 07-1610-8

JOHN, SON OF THUNDER by Ellen Gunderson Traylor. In this saga of adventure, romance, and discovery, travel with John—the disciple whom Jesus loved—down desert paths, through the courts of the Holy City, and to the foot of the cross as he leaves his luxury as a privileged son of Israel for the bitter hardship of his exile on Patmos. 07-1903-4

Other Living Books Best-Sellers

LIFE IS TREMENDOUS! by Charlie "Tremendous" Jones. Believing that enthusiasm makes the difference, Jones shows how anyone can be happy, involved, relevant, productive, healthy, and secure in the midst of a high-pressure, commercialized society. 07-2184-5

LORD, COULD YOU HURRY A LITTLE? by Ruth Harms Calkin. These prayer-poems from the heart of a godly woman trace the inner workings of the heart, following the rhythms of the day and seasons of the year with expectation and love. 07-3816-0

LORD, I KEEP RUNNING BACK TO YOU by Ruth Harms Calkin. In prayer-poems tinged with wonder, joy, humanness, and questioning, the author speaks for all of us who are groping and learning together what it means to be God's child. 07-3819-5

MORE THAN A CARPENTER by Josh McDowell. A hard-hitting book for people who are skeptical about Jesus' deity, his resurrection, and his claim on their lives. 07-4552-3

MOUNTAINS OF SPICES by Hannah Hurnard. Here is an allegory comparing the nine spices mentioned in the Song of Solomon to the nine fruits of the Spirit. A story of the glory of surrender by the author of **Hinds' Feet on High Places.** 07-4611-2

OUT OF THE STORM by Grace Livingston Hill. Gail finds herself afloat on an angry sea, desperately trying to keep an unconscious man from slipping away from her. 07-4778-X

QUICK TO LISTEN, SLOW TO SPEAK by Robert E. Fisher. Families are shown how to express love to one another by developing better listening skills, finding ways to disagree without arguing, and using constructive criticism. 07-5111-6

THE SECRET OF LOVING by Josh McDowell. McDowell explores the values and qualities that will help both single and married readers to be the right person for someone else. He offers a fresh perspective for evaluating and improving the reader's love life. 07-5845-5

Other Living Books Best-Sellers

STRIKE THE ORIGINAL MATCH by Charles Swindoll. Many couples ask: What do you do when the warm, passionate fire that once lit your marriage begins to wane? Here, Chuck Swindoll provides biblical steps for rekindling the fires of romance and building marital intimacy. 07-6445-5

SUCCESS! THE GLENN BLAND METHOD by Glenn Bland. The author shows how to set goals and make plans that really work. His ingredients of success include spiritual, financial, educational, and recreational balances. 07-6689-X

WHAT WIVES WISH THEIR HUSBANDS KNEW ABOUT WOMEN by James Dobson. The best-selling author of **Dare to Discipline** and **The Strong-Willed Child** brings us this vital book that speaks to the unique emotional needs and aspirations of today's woman. An immensely practical, interesting guide. 07-7896-0

WINDOW TO MY HEART by Joy Hawkins. A collection of heartfelt poems aptly expressing common emotions and thoughts that single women of any age experience. The author's vital trust in a loving God is evident throughout. 07-7977-0

If you are unable to find any of these titles at your local bookstore, you may call Tyndale's toll-free number **1-800-323-9400, X-214** for ordering information. Or you may write for pricing to **Tyndale Family Products, P.O. Box 448, Wheaton, IL 60189-0448.**